The Left-Hander's Handbook

THE LEFT-HANDED BOOK

THE NATURAL SUPERIORITY OF THE LEFT-HANDER

THE WORLD'S GREATEST LEFT-HANDERS

LEFT-HANDED KIDS

by
James T.
de Kay

MJF BOOKS
NEW YORK

Published by MJF Books
Fine Communications
Two Lincoln Square
60 West 66th Street
New York, NY 10023

Library of Congress Catalog Card Number 97-72759
ISBN 1-56731-229-2

10   9   8   7   6   5   4   3   2   1

THE
LEFT-HANDED
BOOK

"Left-handers have much
more enthusiasm for life.
They sleep on the wrong
side of the bed, and
their heads become
stagnant on that side."

— Casey Stengel

Dedicated to Alexander the Great,
Benjamin Franklin, Babe Ruth,
Hans Holbein, Betty Grable,
Huntington Hartford, Rock
Hudson, Peter Lawford,
Rudy Vallee, Joanne Woodward,
Casey Stengel, Dick Van Dyke,
Harry S. Truman, Ty Cobb,
Judy Garland, Charlemagne,
Milton Caniff, Pablo Picasso,
King George VI, Lord Nelson,
Bill Mauldin, Carmen Basilio,

and half the Beatles (Paul and Ringo) who are all left-handed, and to Helen and Gareth, who are not.

At least one person in ten
is left-handed.

Dr. Bryng Bryngelson, of the
University of Minnesota, says:
"Left-handed people tend to be
more creative, more imaginative
than right-handed people." Which
may explain why Michaelangelo,
Raphael and Leonardo were
all left-handed.

It doesn't necessarily explain
why Gerald Ford is left-handed.

* "Jerry's the only man I ever knew who can't walk and chew gum at the same time."
— Lyndon Johnson

The human brain is divided
into two hemispheres, and
one dominates the other. If
the right hemisphere dominates,
you'll be left-handed.

Being left-handed in
a right-handed world
can be frustrating,
which may account for
the fact that both
Jack the Ripper and
the Boston Strangler
were left-handed.

This frustration may also
account for the disquieting
statistic that left-handers
are 3 times more apt to
become alcoholics.

Just look
at the
problems
they face…

Left-handed violinists,
guitarists, banjoists,
etc., must restring their
instruments, which are
designed wrong-way to...

...while left-handed
saxophonists
simply do not
exist.

 Gum wrapper openers are right-handed...

...and so are apple corers.
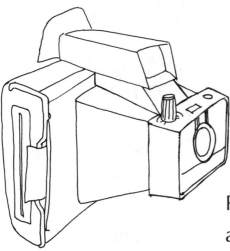

Polaroid cameras are so right-handed it's ridiculous.

Something as simple as a
frying pan

becomes a
real nuisance if
there's only one pouring lip.

It's always on the wrong side.

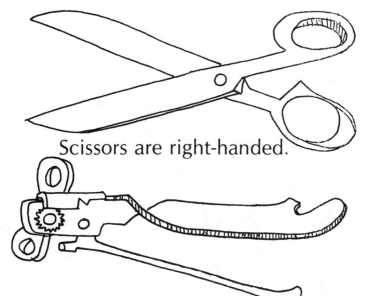

Scissors are right-handed.

Can openers are right-handed.

And so are wrist watches.

A more complicated tool can be a downright menace. This typical power saw, for example. A left-hander must cross his arms to operate it. Since he can't see where he's going, he'll either saw a crooked line, or chop off a couple of fingers.

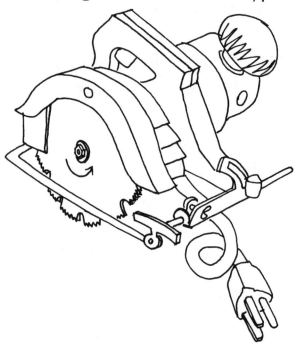

Consider the RIFLE: the
bolt action variety that
bolts the wrong way,

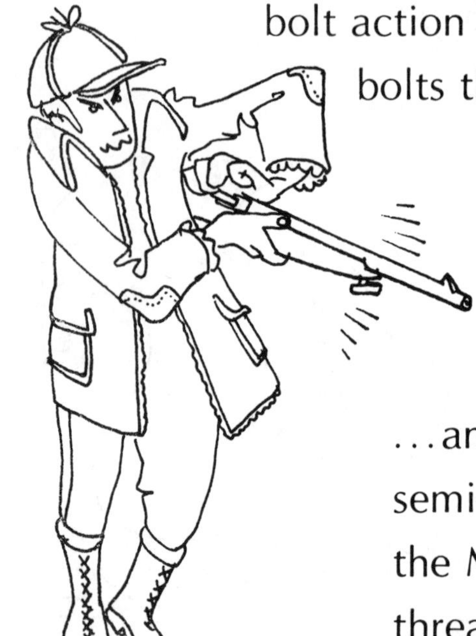

...and the gas-operated
semi-automatics — like
the M-1 — which
threatens to scoop out
your eyeball every
time you fire it
left-handed.

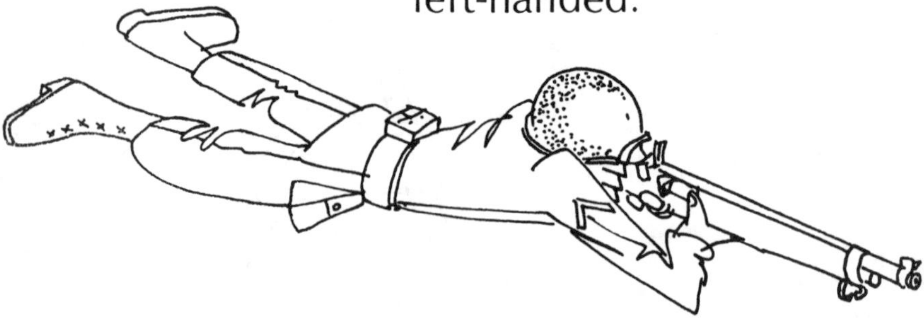

PLAYING CARDS:

Left-handed
full house.

Same hand, considerably
improved by moving it
to the right.

(Are you beginning to get the picture?)

ADDING MACHINES...and SUBTRACTING
MACHINES:

(note position of handle.)

And then there's READING and WRITING:

Left-handers, who make up only 10% of the population, account for almost half the students in remedial reading courses. No one is sure why this is the case, but most experts agree it stems from the fact that in the western world words go left to right.

The less said about left-handed writing, the better.

Why are things so tough on left-handers? Because a lot of people who ought to know better, believe left-handers are an insignificant minority.

H. G. Wells, who CERTAINLY ought to have known better, believed left-handedness was insignificant, **and always had been.** He wrote: "WE KNOW [NEANDERTHAL MEN] WERE RIGHT-HANDED, LIKE MODERN MEN, BECAUSE THE LEFT SIDE OF THE BRAIN...WAS BIGGER THAN THE RIGHT." This is nonsense.

Virtually all of the evidence
shows that in prehistoric times...

THE NUMBER OF
LEFT-HANDERS
JUST ABOUT
EQUALED THE
NUMBER OF
RIGHT-HANDERS!

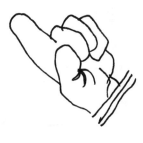

For instance, if Neanderthal men were exclusively right-handed, they would have invented right-handed tools, correct? Instead, they invented **ambidextrous** tools, suitable for either hand:

hammers,   saws,

axes,

pails,   pottery,

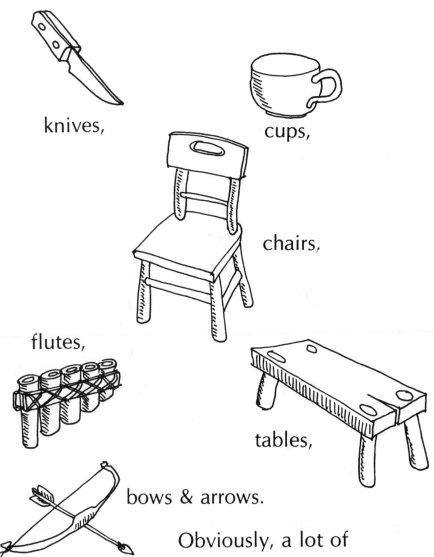

knives,

cups,

chairs,

flutes,

tables,

bows & arrows.

Obviously, a lot of
left-handed Neanderthals
helped design these
clever innovations.

31

Throughout much of ancient
history, the left-handers had
equal rights:

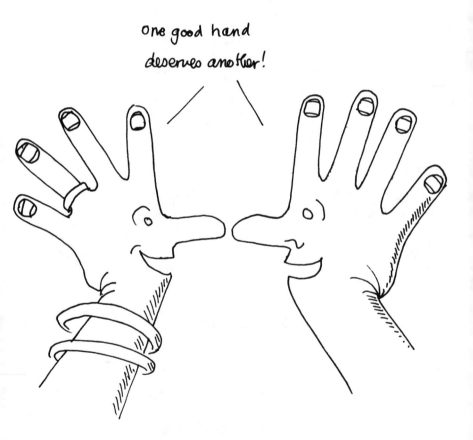

One good hand
deserves another!

This was even true in writing...

The Egyptians didn't feel
they had to write left
to right. They wrote up,
down, left **or** right,
depending on whim.

The Greeks wrote BOUSTROPHEDON style,
with each line alternating down the page,
like an ox plowing a field:
　　first line left to right,
　　next line right to left,
　　then another left to right

etcete

The Chinese, even to this day, write in vertical columns from right to left, which would indicate a slightly left-handed preference.

BIBLICAL NOTE: The Israelites were twice defeated by a Benjaminite army of "700 picked men who were left-handed." So much for you, Mr. H. G. Wells!

Actually, it was the Romans who made up all the rules against left-handers. They were the most militantly right-handed people in history.

Romans invented the
right-handed handshake…

…the fascist salute…

…and that left to right alphabet
that still causes a lot of trouble:

ABCDEFGHI
KLMNOPQ
RSTVWXYZ

The Roman word
for <u>right</u> was:

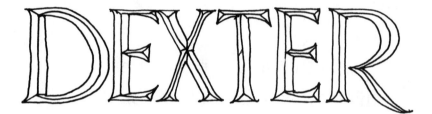

Their word for
<u>left</u> was:

SINISTER

Is it any wonder
left-handedness went
out of style?

In the Dark Ages, after the Roman
Empire collapsed, a lot of people gave
up reading, writing, shaking hands and
saluting, and went back to being left-
handed. Once again, the tools invented
in this period reflect a general
ambidextrality.

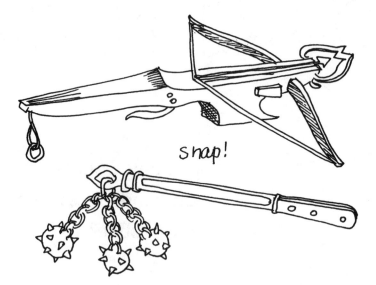

snap!

crackle!

pop!

43

MIDDLE EASTERN FOOTNOTE:
The Arabs have always insisted you
eat with your right hand. This
taboo isn't really directed against
left-handers, but stems solely from
certain social problems that arise
where water is scarce. Some time
back in history, they decided
that the left hand should be
reserved for certain hygienic
purposes, the intensely personal
nature of which made that hand
particularly unsuitable for the
communal dinner pot.

To show their impartiality, Arabs
write left-handedly:

Today, we're right back where we were with the Romans. Just about everything's right-handed. Take jet planes. The pilot sits on this side so he can operate the all-important center control panel.

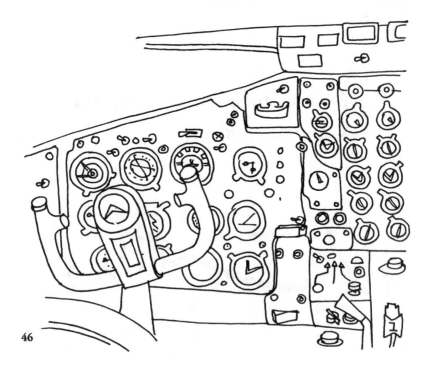

But what if the pilot's left-handed? He'd be more efficient on this side, but he's not allowed to sit here. Is this the safest possible arrangement?

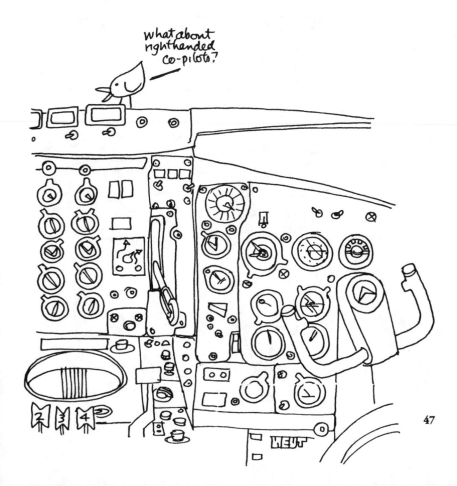

what about righthanded co-pilots?

THIS IS YOUR PILOT, LEFTY JONES...
WE ARE NOW CRUISING AT 30,000 FEET,
AT A SPEED OF...

If everything's so right-handed, wouldn't it make sense to train left-handers to be right-handed? Psychologists say "no"...it makes them stutter and things like that.

So, what's the answer?

A LEFTHANDED

Be it resolved that
all LEFT-THINKING
citizens, mindful that
their BIRTHLEFT
has been denied them,
shall henceforth
stand up for their
LEFTS! We call

MANIFESTO!

upon each one of them to support this BILL OF LEFTS, and specifically to…

BUY LEFT!

Purchase only left-handed products!

Develop a taste for Borden's Cheese Spred... one of the few products with a tear strip that works for left-handers as well as right!

Buy an English car, and get a left-handed gearshift free!

Insist on left-handed
check books!

And buy a typewriter —
the only left-handed
machine in general
use! (Most of
the important
keys are
on the
left.)

Purchase only the works of left-handers!

PLAY LEFT!

Return baseball to its pre-eminence as the great American pastime! (It favors left-handers.)

The lefthanded batter faces first base when he's completed his swing...and has a head start in running out his hit. 32% of all major league batters are lefthanded.

A lefthanded pitcher can
keep an eye on first base
during his wind-up, and
cut down a runner's lead.
30% of all major league
pitchers are southpaws.

The lefthanded first baseman
can cover a tremendous area
of the infield with his right
(gloved) hand. Also, he's got an
advantage throwing to second
for the double play. 48% of all
major league first basemen are
lefthanded.

BUT...
there are
absolutely no
lefthanded
catchers!

Most important…

ACT LEFT!

Don't knuckle under! You've made

enough adjustments!

EAT LEFT! Let the other people

at the counter worry for a change!

RELAX LEFT! If you can't get a

left-handed tool for the job…

forget it!

WRITE LEFT! Write backwards! No one can read it, but with a little practice, you'll find it a lot easier for you!

REMEMBER! There are at least TWENTY MILLION left-handed Americans! Singly, they can do nothing, but UNITED...

...they can change the world!

COMES THE REVOLUTION...

...don't be left out.

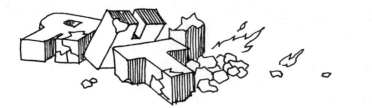

The
Natural Superiority
of
THE
LEFT-HANDER

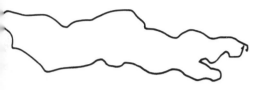

DEDICATED
to the citizens of
LEFT HAND, WEST VIRGINIA

Population 450,
and every one a
Left Hander.

One person in ten is a
left-hander. And every
last one of them thinks
he's sort of special.

Which is
probably
true . . .

No kidding.
Anywhere you look,
left-handedness is
something of a rarity.

Even most plants
are right-handed.
Honeysuckle is one of
the few climbing plants
that twines to the left.

Most flatfish lie down on
their left side. This makes
them right-handed.

The Pacific sand dab is one of the
few that lies down on the other
side. This makes it left-handed.
Or rather, left-finned.

There are even a few sea
shells that curve left-handedly.
They are prized by collectors.

Lobsters are
sometimes
left-han

ded.

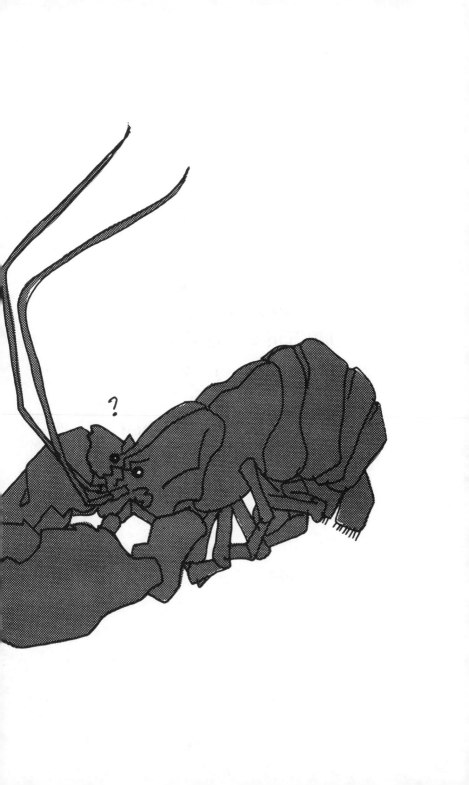

It could be that the
only case where
left-handers are in the
majority is among
gorillas. Their
left arms outweigh their
right, which may
indicate a slight
left-handed bias.
But that's only
speculation.

As far as humans are concerned,
there's evidence that the

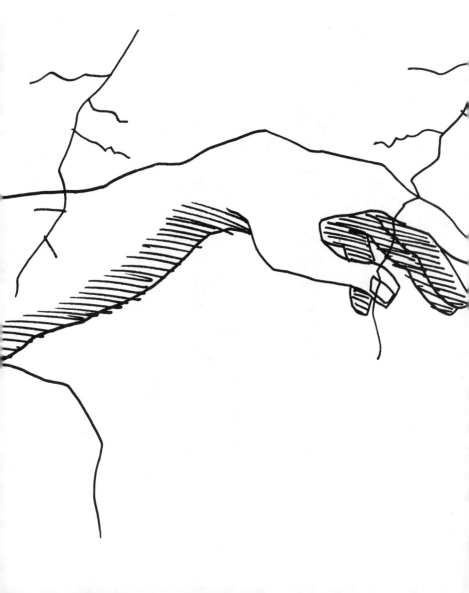

very first member of the
species was left-handed.

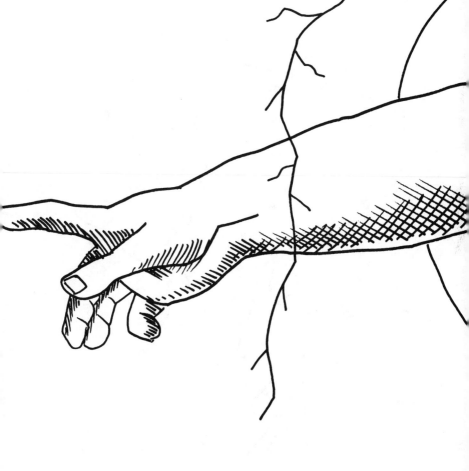

In the early days,
as we know from cave drawings,

There were plenty of
right-handers,
but there were plenty of
left-handers, too.

Things were
fine for
left-handers up
through the
Stone Age.

Look at this
nice left-handed
hammer
I found.

?

But with the
Bronze Age came
manufacturing. And
since most people
were right-handed,
that's the way they
made the tools. To
this day, no one has
ever made a
left-handed sickle.

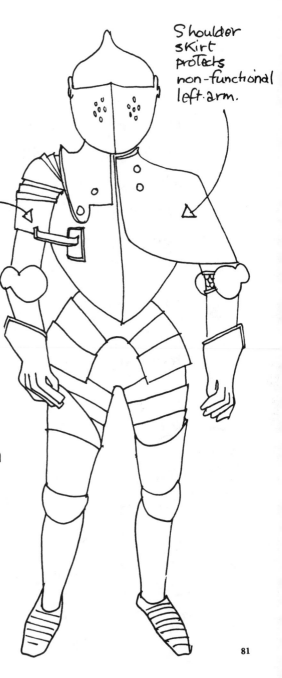

Right-handed lance support

By the
Middle Ages
left-handers
were out in
the cold. Even
suits of
armor were
invariably
right-handed.

That long-ago bias against left-handers is still with us. Bus coin boxes are right-handed.

And so are phonograph tone arms.

Not my Fats Waller 78s.

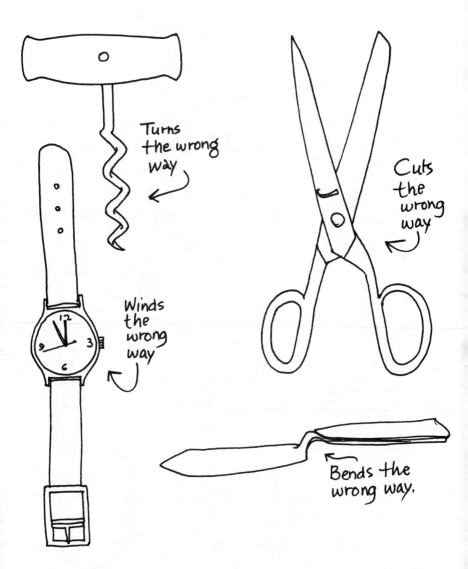

Turns the wrong way

Cuts the wrong way

Winds the wrong way

Bends the wrong way.

It's enough to make left-handers
a little paranoid.

Even
carousels are
right-handed.

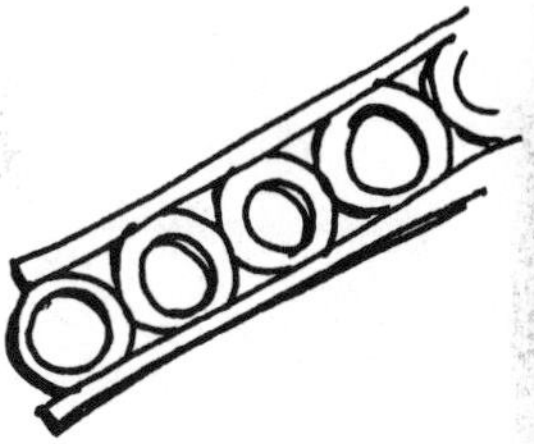

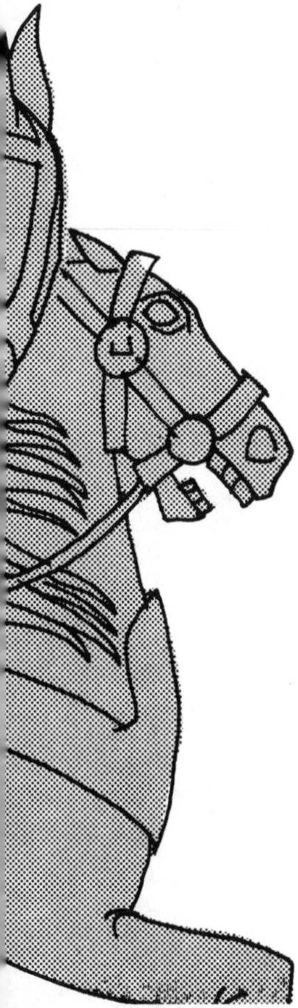

You can't
reach for
the brass
ring with
your left hand.

Today, about the
only thing that
actually favors
left-handers
is the
toll booth.

Of course, if you are a
rich or important
left-hander, you can ignore
all the prejudice.

For instance, it never
bothered Ramses II, who
is always shown as
left-handed.

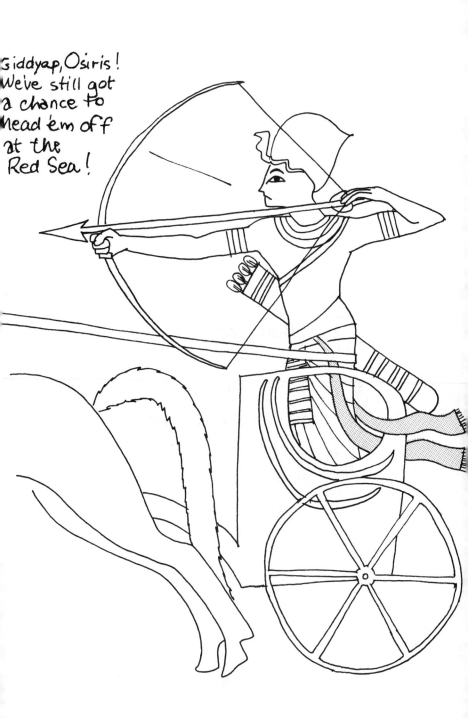

And Ben Franklin
actually gloried in
his left-handedness.
He wrote and published
a treatise in
favor of the
left hand.

I told
you
left-handers
were weird.

James Garfield

Harry Truman

Gerald Ford

There have been three
left-handed Presidents.

And one of them
even had a left-handed
Vice-President.

Gerald Ford, by the way,
may be unique. He is
left-handed only when
sitting down.
He throws a ball, plays golf,
and writes on a blackboard
right-handed.

Jimi Hendrix was neither
rich nor important,
but he became
both by beating
right-handers at their
own game. He restrung
his guitar so he
could play it
left-handed.

In sports, there is often an advantage in left-handedness.

This is particularly true in baseball, which may explain why right-handed players are often ambivalent about left-handers.

In golf, left-handed
Ben Hogan played
right-handed because
he was told the greater
strength in his leading
arm would improve his
stroke.

Years later, he
regretted switching.

Swimming also
favors left-handers.
Neurologists have
shown they adjust
more readily to
underwater vision.
Mark Spitz,
who won
seven Olympic gold
medals, is, as you might
expect, left-handed.

But polo is another story.
It's actually
against the rules to play
left-handed.

And that even goes for
the left-handed
Prince of Wales.

For some reason not quite clear, left-handers make fantastic tennis players. At any given time, about 40% of the top pros are left-handed . . . people like Rod Laver, Jimmy Connors, Manuel Orantes, Guillermo Villas, Martina Navratilova, etc.

Sporting footnote:
In 1890, the baseball
diamond in Chicago was
sited to protect the batters
from the late afternoon
sun. In consequence,
the pitcher faced west,
and if he was left-handed,
he was known as a
southpaw.

Where does
left-handedness
come from?
Is it inherited?
Maybe.

But... can something as rigorously right-handed as the DNA helix actually transmit left-handedness?

We know that if both parents are left-handed, 50% of the kids will be left-handed too.

But if both parents are
right-handed, only 2% of
the kids will be left-handed.

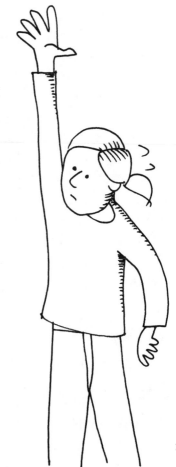

Another indication that
left-handedness is genetic
comes from Scotland's
Kerr family.

For centuries the Kerrs have
been famous for the large number
of left-handers they produce.

They even gave their
castles left-
handed
staircases so they'd be
easy to defend.

At one time,
American Indians
may have been the
world's largest single
population of
left-handers. There's
evidence that
one in three
was left-handed.

The Incas thought
left-handedness was
lucky. One of their
great chiefs was
LLOQUE YUPANQUI,
which means
left-handed.

Inca-dinka-doo.

There's a high incidence of
left-handedness in twins, but it's
rare to find both left-handed.

There are more
left-handed boys than girls.
No one knows why.

Older mothers are more
likely to produce left-handed
children
than younger
mothers.

Some experts claim
they can spot a
left-hander in infancy.
The whorl of their
hair, it is said, will
twist counterclockwise.

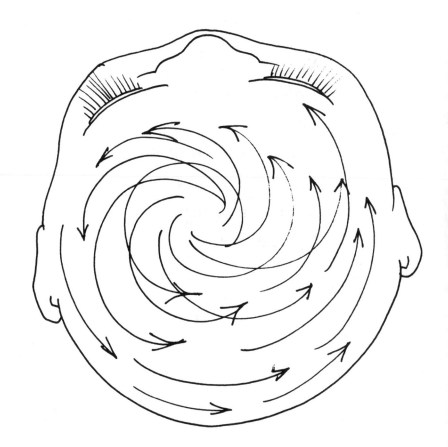

Virtually all
pediatricians will
agree that if a
child has a preference
for the left hand,
it will show up
by age five.

*The New England Journal of
Medicine* suggests you can
tell if you're left-handed
if the base of your left
thumbnail is wider
and squarer than
the right.

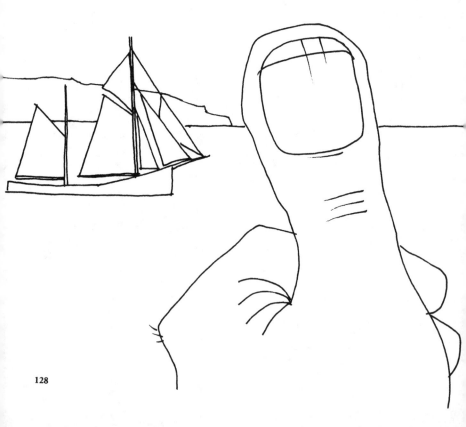

Another researcher,
Theodore Blau, has a
different test. Using
each hand in turn,
draw X's, then circle
them. If you draw the
circles counterclockwise
you're left-handed
(he says).

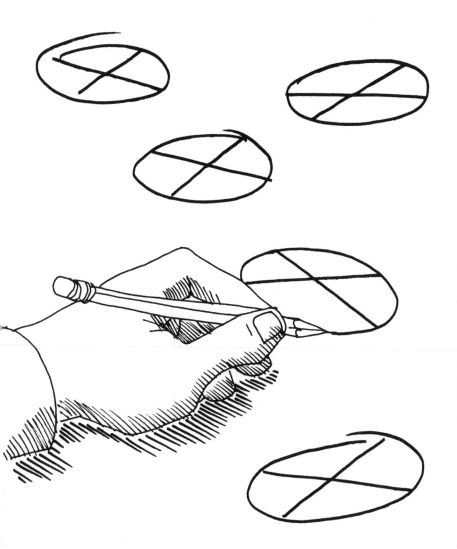

But at least one
authority takes
it beyond the
question of
which hand you
use.

Dr. Samuel Johnson,
who was probably a
closet left-hander,
seems to agree. He was
spooked by left-footedness.

To enter the
house with
the left foot
brings down
evil on the
inmates.

Psychologists are fascinated
with left-handers. They're
constantly studying
them and coming up
with reasons not to
be left-handed.

For example, recent studies by
psychologist Theodore Blau (he
of the counterclockwise circles)
show left-handers
to be . . .

stubborn,

oversensitive,

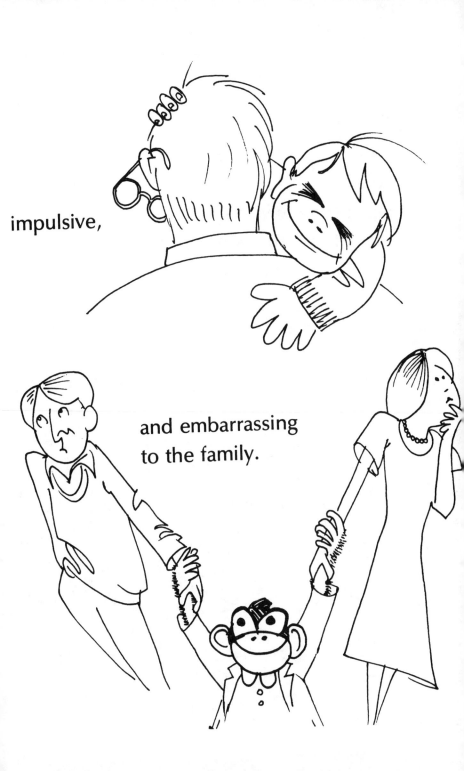

impulsive,

and embarrassing
to the family.

Of course, this kind of
data cuts both ways.
Left-hander Joan of Arc
was certainly impulsive, but
that's how she won battles.

And although Billy the Kid
was almost assuredly one of
those left-handers who
embarrass his family, he is
also without doubt, the
stuff of legend.

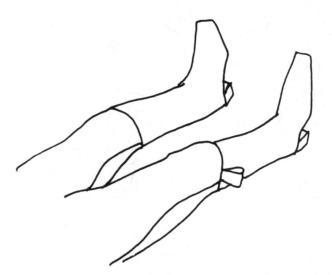

Blau goes on to find that
left-handers have difficulty
following directions.

Go pick up
your room.

And have trouble
completing projects.

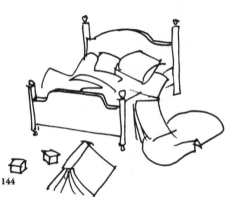

All done!

They're also likely to
have speech problems.

And to top it all off,
Blau claims that
bedwetting
among left-handers
is likely to continue
beyond the age
of three.

Another psychologist
named Blau—Abram
Blau, this time—decided
that left-handers were
just plain anti-social
and deliberately used
the "wrong" hand just
to make a mess and
raise a little hell.

This suggestion of
left-handed deviltry
harks back thousands
of years, to the time
we started throwing
salt over our left
shoulders to propitiate
the fiends who always
lurk—of course—to
the left.

Even good old
Dr. Spock, who
usually recommends
you let your kid
do almost anything,
suggests you
discourage
left-handedness in
young children.

But maybe the final, and wisest, medical opinion on the subject comes from neurosurgeon Joseph Bogan: "Right-handers are a bunch of chocolate soldiers. If you've seen one, you've seen 'em all. But left-handers are something else again."

Well, at least everyone
agrees left-handers are special.
But are they specially good?

Or specially bad?

To find out, we must
enter a very strange world . . .
the world of the human
brain . . . a shadowy place of
surprises and contradictions,

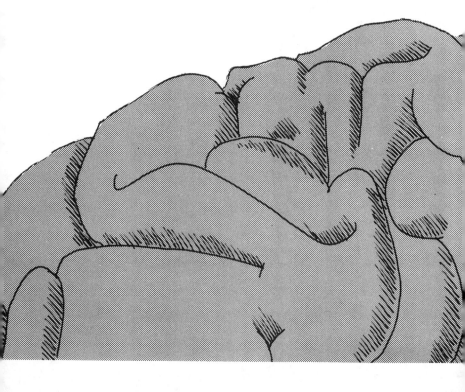

only partially mapped and imperfectly understood. But we know it holds the key to the secret of left-handedness.

The brain is made up of two
very different hemispheres. We
need both, but for different
reasons, since each has its
own functions . . .

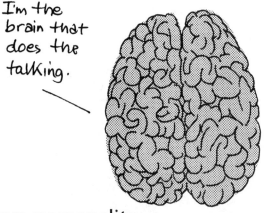

its own personality . . .

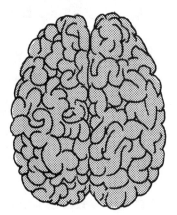

its own specialties . . .

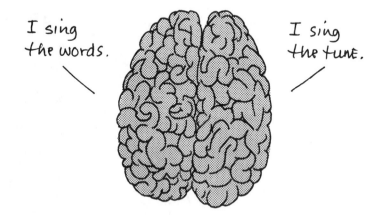

I sing
the words.

I sing
the tune.

and most significantly, in reference to
the subject under consideration,
its own hand.

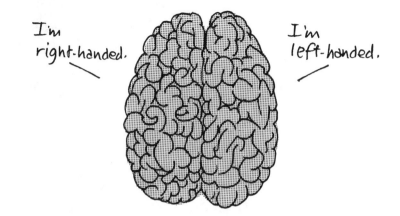

I'm
right-handed.

I'm
left-handed.

Hey! I'm in charge here! It stands to reason! I'm the responsible one!

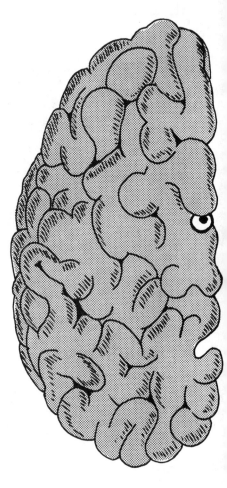

Because they have such different points of view,

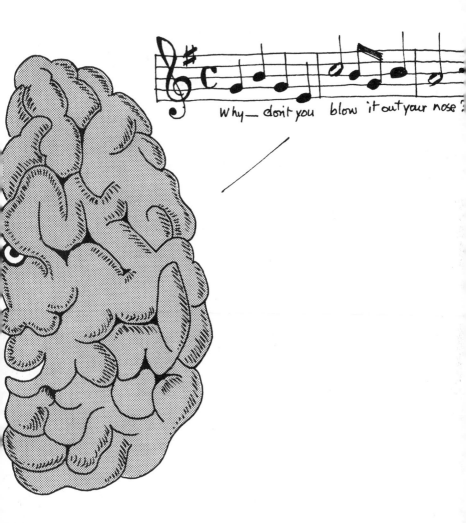

the "thinking" and "feeling" hemispheres compete for dominance.

Generally speaking, people with a dominant "thinking" brain become right-handed.

It seems only reasonable!

While those with a
dominant "feeling" brain
become left-handed.

I'm absolutely
over COME!

You might expect a
right-hander to be verbal,
analytical, and good at math.

So I unload
United Federal
in a short
position, while
recognizing that
Amalgamated
Could crossruff
my ITD before
Uncle Sam got his
greedy mitts on it...

And a left-hander to be
intuitive, and mystical, with
a strong visual sense.

Which is exactly the case.

In politics, maybe this is
why cold, heartless conservatives
are called right-wingers.

And why dreamy, bleeding heart
liberals are called left-wingers.

A lot of hard
evidence shows that
most left-handers—
because they are
dominated by a different
kind of brain—are
a distinctly different
kind of people.

They literally think
differently, even when
solving the same problem as
a right-hander.

Right-handers adapt
comfortably to
abstractions.

But left-handers tend to
translate everything
into visual imagery.

Right-handers tend to
think lineally, linking
their ideas in logical order.

And therefore,
m'lord,
whereas the
party of the
first part...

Left-handers are more apt
to think holistically, skipping
over the details.

Which explains why so many creative people have been left-handed.

Edward R. Murrow

H.G. Wells

Pablo Picasso

Anthony Newley

Ronald Searle

Leonardo

Michaelangelo

Murray Skurnik

Paul Williams

Peter Benchley

Jim Bishop

Paul Klee

Milton Caniff

Hans Holbein

Clarence Darrow

And why left-handers
seem almost to dominate
show business.

Greta
Garbo

Charlie
Chaplin

Marcel
Marceau

Glen
Campbell

Richard
Pryor

George
Burns

Telly Savalas

Lenny
Bruce

Shirley
MacLaine

Rex
Harrison

Michael
Landon

Jim
Henson

Robert
De Niro

Marilyn Monroe

And perhaps most
interesting of all, it
helps explain one of
the more intriguing
statistics of the space age.
When NASA
went searching for the
kind of imaginative,
super-reliable, multitalented
people they would
need to explore
the moon . . .

. . . one out of every four Apollo astronauts turned out to be left-handed— a figure

greater than statistical probability.

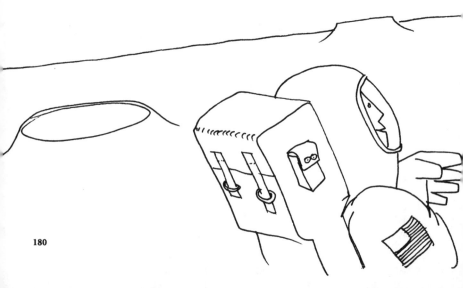

Far from being society's misfits, data like this suggests that left-handers are almost a different species. Who knows? Maybe they're the next step up in evolution.

In any case, we now
know why left-handers
have always believed
they were special.

In their hearts, they know
they're right.

THE WORLD'S GREATEST LEFT-HANDERS

WHY LEFT-HANDERS ARE JUST PLAIN BETTER THAN EVERYBODY ELSE

JAMES T. de KAY and SANDY HUFFAKER

If you are left-handed, this book is dedicated to you.
If you aren't, eat your heart out.

Left-hders are a different breed . . .

TYPICAL
RIGHT-HANDER

They really are.

TYPICAL
LEFT-HANDER

THE BRAIN

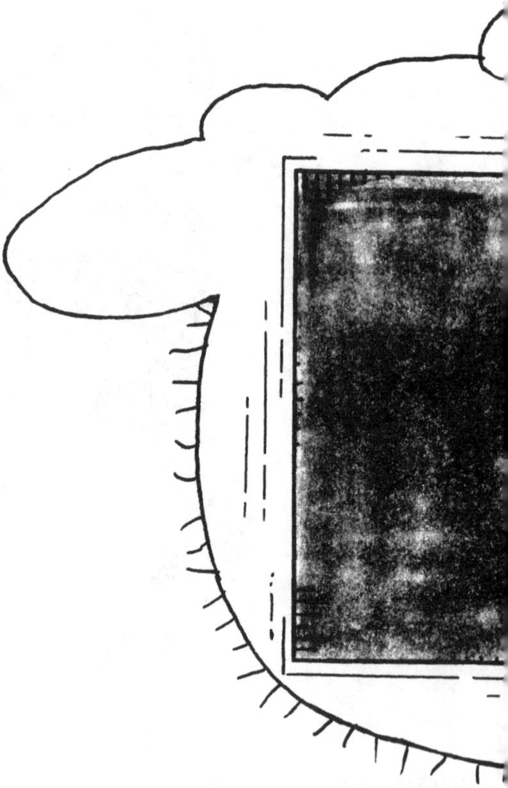

Right-handers are wired
into the logical half of the
brain, which makes them
sensible,
reasonable,
and dull.

(AERIAL VIEW)

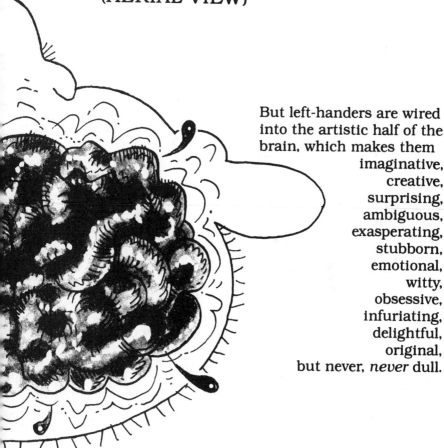

But left-handers are wired into the artistic half of the brain, which makes them
imaginative,
creative,
surprising,
ambiguous,
exasperating,
stubborn,
emotional,
witty,
obsessive,
infuriating,
delightful,
original,
but never, *never* dull.

The goofy, unpredictable nature of left-handers is why so many of them turn out to be great achievers, including the assortment of saints, scalawags, heroes, wackos, and geniuses in the following pages. . . .

☞ BUZZ ALDRIN

The record of left-handers in the space program is highly significant. Of the twelve astronauts who actually walked on the moon, four were left-handed. That's one in three, compared to a national average of one left-hander in ten. Obviously left-handers, with their recognized capacity for original thought, intuition, and self-reliance, are particularly suited to the rigors of space travel.

Buzz Aldrin was the first of the left-handers on the moon, His initial task, after climbing from the lunar module, was to take a picture of his captain, Neil Armstrong, with a Hasselblad camera—one of the most right-handed bits of machinery ever invented.

ALEXANDER THE GREAT

Left-handedness is more than just a physical specialization. It's a state of mind. And no example proves it better than one of the earliest recorded left-handers, Alexander of Macedon. He was a warrior, visionary, world leader, and crybaby, all wrapped up in a single, immensely complicated package. In a lifetime of only thirty-three years he created the first modern empire, invented snorkel diving, designed the first planned city, and cut the Gordian knot, whatever that was.

His like will never be seen again because, like all left-handers, he was a true original.

CARL PHILIPP EMANUEL BACH

Johann Sebastian Bach had twenty children, many of whom made a living in the music business. By far the most successful was his second son, the left-handed C.P.E. Bach, whose compositions were actually more popular than his father's (Johann Sebastian was not amused).

It's likely that quite a number of Bach's family were left-handed (the trait is closely related to musical talent), but Germanic culture has always been strongly biased against the left hand, and C.P.E. may have been the only Bach who wasn't forcibly switched to right-handedness. Although switching has been shown to cause serious psychological consequences (including stammering), it is still common in Germany, although it has largely disappeared elsewhere.

F. LEE BAILEY

One wouldn't expect left-handers to make great lawyers, since the law is based on logic, and logic is a right-handed characteristic. But the left-handed F. Lee Bailey is a highly successful lawyer precisely because of his left-handed character. His left-handed skepticism helps him see beyond the obvious; his close ties to his emotions help him establish empathy with jurors; and his obsessiveness keeps him looking for fresh angles and clues, no matter how lost the cause may seem.

Rule of thumb: for ordinary matters get a right-handed lawyer, but if you're really in trouble look for a left-hander.

PETER BENCHLEY

The author of *Jaws* may be the most determinedly right-handed left-hander on record. The fact is, Peter Benchley favors his right hand for virtually all activities—playing tennis, throwing a ball, hammering a nail, etc. The only exception is writing, which he does left-handedly. To a neurologist this makes him left-handed. He may be right-handed at virtually everything else, but the act of writing is so difficult, so complex, so significant a skill that it far outweighs any other manifestation of handedness. If you write left-handed, you *are* left-handed, and that's that.

☞ 700 BENJAMITES

The Bible is militantly right-handed and takes every opportunity to equate left-handedness with evil (literally, a lack of righteousness). The sole exception to this prejudice seems to be in the Book of Judges, which includes the story of the seven hundred left-handed Benjamites who chased the Israelite army off the field of battle.

The Arabs have been trying to learn their secret for years.

☞ BILLY THE KID

The murderous William H. Bonney, who was born in Brooklyn, had shot twenty-one men by the time he was twenty-one years old. And he killed them all left-handedly. Chances are he was left-eyed as well, because he had to be a good shot to compile a record like that. (You can be left-eyed, left-eared, and left-footed as well as left-handed. It's usually more efficient to keep your dominances on the same side of the body.)

Billy died in New Mexico before he was twenty-two, which is probably why he's still known as Billy the Kid instead of Billy the Grown-up.

☞ THE BOSTON STRANGLER

Albert DeSalvo, the Boston Strangler, is an example of left-handedness where the craziness got out of hand. He terrified an entire city and compiled one of the most horrifying records of murder and rape in history.

In the nineteenth century, criminologists believed left-handedness was a sure sign of degeneracy and evil. Today we may laugh at such naïveté, but when one looks at DeSalvo's frightening record, we have to acknowledge that, at least in part, they may have been on to something.

☞ CAROL BURNETT

You'd think left-handers would be a pretty gloomy bunch, considering the number of booby traps the world sets out for them—right-handed scissors, right-handed golf clubs, right-handed can openers, etc. But instead of crying about their fate, left-handers are more likely to turn into comedians. Carol Burnett is only one of a long, long list of distinguished left-handers who make a living by making you laugh.

Why so many left-handed comics? There seems to be something goofy about the way they look at the world. Maybe they see it a little more clearly.

LEWIS CARROLL

Charles Dodgson, who called himself Lewis Carroll and created Alice in Wonderland, exhibits all the earmarks of a left-hander switched to right-handedness: stammering, extreme shyness, and a sort of controlled dyslexia that takes the form of punning and other word play, mirror writing, and a kind of humor that depends on spectacularly unreasonable reasoning.

Certainly *Through the Looking-Glass*, with its wrong-way-around orientation, its loony logic, and its mind-warping Jabberwocky, is the greatest left-handed masterpiece in literature.

CHARLIE CHAPLIN

And then there's Charlie Chaplin. With a cane, a pasted-on moustache, and a few bits of clothing picked up from Mack Sennett's wardrobe, he created a character that can still bring tears of laughter to the world.

Significantly, the left-handed brain is not only unpredictable (which is why it's so comical), but also nonverbal (which is why Chaplin and several other people in this book managed to communicate so well without words).

CHARLEMAGNE

Charlemagne was King of the Franks and eventually the first Emperor in Western Europe. He did all the things expected of a great leader: he fought wars, gave parties, and fooled around with women.

He was also illiterate, which suited his left-handedness just fine. Left-handers have always had trouble with our left-to-right style of writing (they can't see what they've written until they take their hand away). Being illiterate gave Charlemagne more time to fight, party, and fool around with women.

TY COBB

Like most great baseball players, Ty Cobb was left-handed, and like most left-handers, he was a little kooky. It was rumored that he used to sharpen his spikes before each game so he could cut up the defending fielder when he slid foot first into a base. Whether the rumor is true or not, a lot of players must have believed it, because he managed to steal a total of 892 bases.

Appropriately, since baseball is such a left-handed game, Ty Cobb was the first player ever elected to the Hall of Fame, in 1936.

JIMMY CONNORS

Tennis has traditionally been a magnet for left-handers, and recently they have come to dominate both the men's and women's divisions. The terrible-tempered Jimmy Connors, who has insulted umpires and ball boys on five continents, is typical of the breed.

Just why so many left-handers should be drawn to tennis probably stems from the fact that left-handers tend (a) to be loners rather than team players, and (b) to have particularly well developed space perception. Tennis, with its need for individual action and precise aim, fits them to a T.

GENTLEMAN JIM CORBETT

The man who won the heavyweight crown from the great John L. Sullivan in New Orleans in 1892 did so primarily with the aid of his left fist. Corbett remained the only great left-handed prizefighter until Carmen Basilio came on the scene in 1955. The fact that left-handers have not distinguished themselves to any great extent in the manly art of self-defense does not necessarily mean they are cowardly by nature. But it may indicate an innate lack of bellicosity.

JOHN DILLINGER

During the years of Prohibition, when crooks were a dime a dozen, the left-handed John Dillinger stood out for his style and brio. The FBI labeled him Public Enemy Number One, and he obliged by robbing banks and shooting people in ever greater numbers. (He once wrote a letter to Henry Ford praising the reliability of Ford's new Model A, which he endorsed as a getaway car.)

The fact that bank vaults and tommy guns are right-handed shows that Dillinger had to overcome considerable difficulties to master his trade.

BOB DYLAN

Musical composition came incredibly easily to Bob Dylan, the left-handed singer. He wrote the intensely melodic tune to "Blowin' in the Wind" in less than five minutes, while the words took him almost a month of effort.

As noted elsewhere, the left-handed brain handles music effortlessly but is apt to have some difficulty with language.

☞ M. C. ESCHER

Mathematicians, critics, and teenagers are all admirers of the drawings and engravings of M. C. Escher, the remarkable Dutch artist who could convince you that water flowed upstream and architecture had four dimensions. Escher attributed his highly specialized skills to his left-handedness.

The Escher engravings, found today everywhere from textbooks to T-shirts, demonstrate a highly logical form of illogic, an intellectual approach to the impossible, a fascination with alternative worlds. They also represent a highly civilized horselaugh, which is the left-handed brain in action.

GERALD FORD

Gerald Ford got labeled as a klutz so early in his administration that few people noticed that he was a pretty good President. Instead, the public was fed a sequence of photographs showing him tripping on the stairs, bumping into things, and generally getting in his own way. To be fair, clumsiness *is* an aspect of left-handedness (in spite of all the great southpaw athletes), but even his enemies agree the left-handed Ford got a bum rap from the press.

BENJAMIN FRANKLIN

The left-handedness of America's greatest wit, diplomat, scientist, and publisher helped him in his early career as a printer, because left-handers come naturally to a very unusual skill: the ability to read and write backwards. In Franklin's day a printer had to set type by hand, and it was a distinct asset to be able to read the type, which was, of course, in reverse.

This backwards-reading skill, which all typesetters pick up, comes easily to left-handers, who have an innate preference for reading right to left. The tendency to read the wrong way accounts for the large number of left-handed dyslexics.

☞ GRETA GARBO

Greta Garbo, the greatest movie star of all time, was most famous for a single line of dialogue: "I vant to be alone." The line relates to her reclusive nature—she was always painfully shy—and also to her left-handedness. In general, because the left-handed brain is nonverbal, left-handers are often not good talkers and are apt to avoid social contact.

Garbo, who established herself before talking films, is one of the many left-handers who were superb silent communicators.

JAMES A. GARFIELD

James A. Garfield holds the distinction of being America's first left-handed President. Unfortunately, he did not hold the distinction for long, since he managed to get in the way of an assassin's bullet soon after his election in 1880, and served only seven months in office. Today he is primarily remembered through his namesake, a large, overweight cat who beats up on dogs and eats lasagna.

JUDY GARLAND

For some thirty years, Judy Garland reigned supreme as one of the world's greatest singers and actresses. From child star to torch singer, she touched hearts around the world in a way that has never been equaled. The fact that she was left-handed helps explain how she was able to project such a remarkable sense of fragility and vulnerability, because these are characteristics of the slightly out-of-phase nature of left-handers.

URI GELLER

Uri Geller continues to fascinate people by bend-
ing spoons, etc., using only sheer mental concentra-
tion. Whether the left-handed Geller is a charlatan
or a natural wonder, his mental gymnastics are typical of left-handed thinking. . . . Unorthodox ways
of thought are absolutely standard among left-
handers.

GEORGE VI

King George VI, one of the multitudinous left-handed members of British royalty (his widow, Elizabeth, the Queen Mother, is also left-handed, as is their grandson the Prince of Wales), was trained into right-handedness as a child. As a direct result, he suffered from a serious s-s-s-peech imp-p-pediment his entire life.

Luckily, his unfortunate disability did not preclude him from finding gainful employment as an adult.

WHOOPI GOLDBERG

Whoopi Goldberg may be the only Oscar win-
ner named after a cushion. That would be reason
enough to qualify her as one of the great left-
handers, but she has such a dazzling off-the-
wall personality she'd have made the list even if
her name was Jane Doe. It's the surprise factor
that makes left-handers so interesting, and with
Whoopi, her unpredictability is clearly of world
class proportions.

☞ CARY GRANT

In the film *Night and Day*, Cary Grant played the part of Cole Porter. Since Cole Porter was short, lame, and American, while Cary Grant was tall, fit, and English, he was obviously picked for the role because, like Porter, he was left-handed.

Except for the fact that he *is* left-handed, there is nothing particularly left-handed about Cary Grant's personality except, perhaps, for his devastating charm.

JIMI HENDRIX

Jimi Hendrix took his left-handedness lightly. He would either restring a right-handed guitar so he could play it left-handedly, or he'd play a right-handed guitar upside down without restringing it, or he'd play it backwards. He didn't care, and anyway, his wah-wah pedal was just as important as the guitar. He was a master musician, one of the many left-handed ones.

JIM HENSON

It takes a very special kind of person to create something as unique as the Muppets—someone with a gift of fantasy, humor, visual imagination, and that very special duality of personality that lets them be simultaneously themselves and another character. Not surprisingly, the man who fits that description and did in fact create the Muppets, Jim Henson, is left-handed.

It's worth noticing that Kermit the Frog, his first and foremost Muppet, is also left-handed (check the way he holds the banjo).

☞ BEN HOGAN

When the left-handed Ben Hogan started playing golf as a kid in Texas, he had to swing right-handed with a set of clubs borrowed from a friend. As he began to make a name for himself in the sport, he considered switching to left-handed clubs, but was dissuaded by "experts" who told him that his natural left-handedness gave his right-handed swing extra power. He took their advice, but years later, after his retirement, he regretted that he hadn't made the switch in his youth.

☞ REGGIE JACKSON

Left-hander Reggie Jackson's quick wit and high style are known to millions of people who wouldn't know first base from a bass fiddle. His battles with club owners, sportswriters, and even fans fill the newspapers.

Baseball has always made room for mavericks like Jackson, probably because it needs so many left-handers, and if it didn't accept the oddballs, there wouldn't be enough left-handers to spread around.

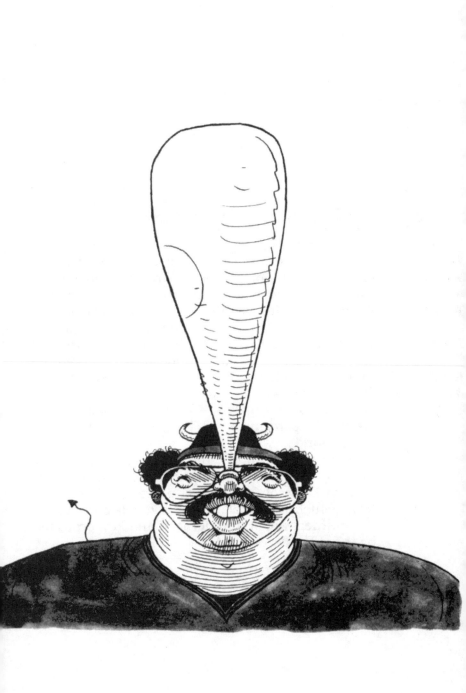

☞ JACK THE RIPPER

When the precarious balance of the left-handed brain goes out of whack, the results can be disastrous—witness Jack the Ripper, the terror of Victorian London. All his victims were women, murdered with identical mutilations, clearly of a psychosexual nature. Who was he? Scotland Yard had only one clue: the knife wounds clearly showed the Ripper was left-handed. The clue was significant, for in nineteenth-century England only 2 percent of the population was left-handed (compared to around 10 percent today). Even so, the Ripper was never found.

Interestingly enough, the case was never closed. Recently suspicion has come to rest on the left-handed Duke of Clarence, grandson of Queen Victoria, which may explain why the police records of the murders are still under lock and key, protected by the Official Secrets Act.

☞ JOAN OF ARC

Joan of Arc heard voices. This unschooled peasant girl believed she could save France, and she convinced the King to give her control of his army. Miraculous? Sure, but also very left-handed. Both the hearing of internal voices and the strong feelings of invincible superiority are closely associated with the left-handed brain. Further proof of Joan's left-handedness is that the only contemporary sketch of her shows her holding her sword in her left hand.

☞ LEONARDO DA VINCI

There are left-handers and there are left-handers. And then there's Leonardo da Vinci, who was so left-handed he needs some special category of his own. He is the patron saint of the breed, and with good reason. He not only invented left-handed machines, painted left-handed masterpieces, and created left-handed statues, he also wrote left-handed—that is, he wrote backwards, from right to left, because that's the sensible way for a left-hander to do it. Of course, this mirror writing was a little difficult for other people to read, but Leo couldn't have cared less.

☞ SHIRLEY MacLAINE

Oscar-winner Shirley MacLaine gives evidence of her left-handedness at every turn. She's a dancer (left-handers have a special thing about music). She's a best-selling writer (left-handers are naturally creative). And she's spent the better part of her life portraying an astonishing parade of kooks (and no one understands kooks better than left-handers).

MARCEL MARCEAU

It's not surprising that the world's greatest mime is left-handed. Indeed, it would be surprising if he weren't. Marcel Marceau's left-handed brain may be nonverbal, but it can speak volumes with the twitch of an eyebrow, a shrug, or the curl of a lip. As he and the other left-handed mimes in this book will attest, if you've got something to say, words may be the least effective way to express it.

☞ HARPO MARX

The Marx Brothers' comedy trademark was uproarious anarchy, and while madness might emanate from any one of them, it was the left-handed Harpo who was undoubtedly the maddest of the bunch. He was, of course, the nonverbal one, too, using his left-handed body language to drown out Groucho and Chico.

PAUL McCARTNEY

Paul McCartney, who plays bass left-handedly and can write a hit song as easily as most people cross the street, is something of a left-handed puzzle. Certainly his handedness and his music go together, but McCartney also exhibits characteristics almost never found in left-handers, including a high degree of business sophistication and a reasonableness and level-headedness generally associated with right-handers. Somehow he breaks the pattern, but perhaps he is proof of just how different left-handers can be . . . even from each other.

MICHELANGELO BUONARROTI

Like Leonardo, Michelangelo is another of those left-handed Florentine artists who seemed to dominate the Italian Renaissance. He's further proof of the strong artistic influence of the left-handed brain: the visionary who could comprehend and solve the enormous technical problems of St. Peter's dome, as well as the obsessive personality who could spend nearly four years flat on his back painting the ceiling.

☞ MARILYN MONROE

There were other, more beautiful movie stars and other, greater actresses. Her list of screen credits is remarkably short of distinguished films. But decades after her death by sleeping pills, Marilyn Monroe continues to cast a spell, to capture the imagination of millions. Whatever she had—and she certainly had something—is impossible to define with any precision, other than to say it was unique.

The fact that she was left-handed—that she shared the sometimes fragile, kooky, surprising nature common to left-handedness—is an important clue to this remarkable woman.

☞ NAPOLEON BONAPARTE

Napoleon never seemed to know what to do with his right hand, and kept it stuck in his vest for the most part. Some people figured he was scratching fleas, but the fact was he was left-handed (although he'd been switched as a child).

His left-handed character surfaced in his quirky imagination, his astonishing vision, his brilliant insight, and his harebrained scheme to conquer Russia.

☞ MARTINA NAVRATILOVA

Wimbledon champion Navratilova is another of those left-handers who dominate world tennis. Left-handedness is twice as common among males as among females, which may account for the fact that Martina has fewer left-handed competitors than do Connors, McEnroe, etc.

☞ VISCOUNT HORATIO NELSON

The left-handed Lord Nelson is perhaps history's greatest naval officer, known for his daring, his imagination, and his ability to surprise the enemy. But before we credit all his genius to his left-handedness, it should be noted that he came by it the hard way: he was by nature right-handed, but switched over when his right arm was blown off in the Battle of Tenerife.

☞ PELÉ

Edson Arantes do Nascimento, the great Brazilian soccer player better known as Pelé, is left-handed. This fact may not seem particularly significant in a sport where you aren't allowed to handle the ball, but what makes it important is that he's also left-footed (most left-handers are) and can kick from the port side with a strength and accuracy most players can't even manage from starboard.

COLE PORTER

At an early age, Cole Porter showed a strong preference for doing things left-handedly. Fortunately, the young Cole had enlightened parents who didn't try to switch him to right-handedness. As a result he grew up and wrote lots of hit songs, including "I Get a Kick Out of You," "Boola-Boola," and "You're the Top."

The left-handed brain is the center of both the sense of rhythm and the perception of pitch, which explains why so many composers and musicians are left-handed.

RICHARD PRYOR

Almost every good comedian is highly complex, and Richard Pryor is one of the best and one of the most complicated. It's not surprising he's left-handed, too. His ambiguous personality (sometimes he plays the frightened tough guy, sometimes he's just the opposite—the vengeful coward), combined with a wildly funny sense of the ridiculous, marks him as a typically outrageous, unpredictable, original left-hander.

☞ RAMSES II

The left-handed Pharaoh Ramses II, who built temples and monuments to himself from Karnak to Abu Simbel, is best remembered for turning a deaf ear to the requests of Moses. As a result, his kingdom suffered a series of misfortunes including a plague of locusts, an inundation of frogs, an epidemic of boils, and various other inconveniences. Finally, to top it all off, his entire army was drowned in the Red Sea.

Stubbornness, to the point of downright unreasonableness is often characteristic of left-handers.

☞ DON RICKLES

Insulting, vicious, libelous, and vulgar pretty well sum up the wit and wisdom of Don Rickles, although it's only fair to add that he is wildly funny as well. When you note he is left-handed, it's easy enough to figure where he gets his talent.

The left-handed brain's sense of humor is immense. (The right-handed brain has no sense of humor whatsoever.)

BABE RUTH

The left-handed George Herman Ruth was a prodigious athlete, probably one of the most highly tuned sportsmen in history. (His eyesight was so keen he could read a phonograph label spinning at 78 rpm.) He could have made it in any sport of his choice. But Ruth chose baseball, or rather it chose him, because it is the one sport that is actually designed to favor left-handers. He started as a pitcher, where his left-handedness allowed him to keep an eye on a runner at first base. When he switched to the outfield so he could bat more often, his handedness gave him an edge at home plate, too. Whenever he hit a ball, he was already a step closer to first base than a right-handed batter. The rest is history.

☞ HELEN HOOVEN SANTMYER

She began her work in the 1920s in the obscurity of an Ohio village. Fifty years later, in 1984, she completed her 1,344-page novel called *And Ladies of the Club . . .* and the Book-of-the-Month Club snapped it up.

Helen Hooven Santmyer's character is as left-handed as they come. Determined to the point of obsession, creative to the point of exhaustion, she is a social chronicler of wit and precision. If she is somewhat less known than many of the others in this book, her achievement is every bit as significant as those of her more famous brothers and sisters of the left.

☞ NORMAN SCHWARZKOPF

General Schwarzkopf's left-handedness is one reason he's got so many stars on his uniform. A good military commander has to be able to see the battle from many different points of view simultaneously—he has to perceive the constantly changing capabilities of his different units, grasp what the enemy is up to, and understand the problems facing the soldiers, sailors, and fliers under his command. Because the general's left-handed brain thinks holistically, he can make all sorts of different judgement calls simultaneously. In the war with Iraq, the bombs were smart, but the commander was smarter.

☞ MARK SPITZ

Mark Spitz, who won seven gold medals in the 1972 Olympics, represents a very special aspect of left-handedness: its strong relationship to swimming.

The left-handed brain is the seat of visual perception and spacial analysis, which means left-handers are apt to have a better than average sense of sight. Water sports require extra work on the part of the eyes, which must constantly adjust to the radically different optical conditions above and below the surface. Since left-handers can handle this problem with greater ease, they are more apt to be drawn to water sports. Their small but real advantage accounts for the high percentage of left-handers on high school and college swimming teams.

☞ CASEY STENGEL

It's absolutely true. One day in Brooklyn, after he was booed by the crowd, Casey Stengel tipped his cap, and a bird flew out of it. And if that isn't a left-handed gesture, nothing is.

After his playing days were over, he managed the Yankees to a string of World Series championships, which even a right-hander might have accomplished, but he then topped his career by leading the Mets to a major league record of 120 losses in 1962, a feat that only a left-hander could have accomplished. He once explained, "Left-handers have much more enthusiasm for life. They sleep on the wrong side of the bed, and their heads become stagnant on that side."

HARRY S. TRUMAN

Harry Truman was a maverick, totally unpredictable and a constant source of surprise. He started out as a ward heeler in a particularly unsavory Kansas City political machine and rose to become an incorruptible senator and then an outstanding President.

He was a left-handed wacko when he used his high office to threaten a local music critic who panned his daughter's singing, and he was a left-handed visionary when he developed the Marshall Plan to save Western Europe.

Imagination, unpredictability, and a distinctive informality—all hallmarks of the left-handed—reached classic proportions in the thirty-third President.

☞ RUDY VALLEE

Rudy Vallee, who carried on a blatantly open love affair with himself for over forty years of public life, was a left-handed singer, bandleader, and movie star. His ego was legend. He once petitioned the city of Los Angeles to get the street that he lived on renamed "Rue de Vallee," but the city fathers didn't share his adoration of himself, and the name of Sunset Boulevard remained unchanged.

Probably his weirdest accomplishment was mastering the saxophone, which is the most decidedly right-handed musical instrument in general use.

☞ DICK VAN DYKE

Like so many other left-handers, Dick Van Dyke built a career on comedy, but in recent years he's taken a more serious tack and devoted a lot of effort to spearheading a national campaign against alcoholism. For reasons not yet fully understood, left-handers are three times more likely than right-handers to suffer from this condition, and Van Dyke is out to prove that it's no laughing matter.

QUEEN VICTORIA

The high proportion of left-handers in the British royal family (you'll find several scattered through these pages) can be traced to Queen Victoria, who was herself left-handed but was switched in childhood. It has been the heavy documentation of the royal family over the generations—the endless court records, diaries, memoirs, and official histories, which have included all sorts of details including handedness of various siblings and cousins—that has provided scientists with the chief evidence to support the argument that left-handedness is inheritable, and therefore of a genetic nature.

Thanks to Victoria, we know that left-handers are born, not made.

LEFT-HANDED KIDS

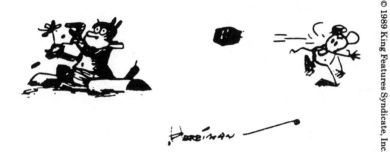

Dedicated to
COLIN DAWKINS
who first told me
that most Krazy Kats
are left-handed, and
Ignatz Mouses aren't.

Left-handed kids tend
to be . . . well, a little different.

A little messier . . .

. . . a little dreamier . . .

. . . a little more emotional.

They're also likely to
be a little smarter
than right-handers.

Left-handers are twice
as likely to qualify for
membership in Mensa,
the high-IQ society.

Left-handers often do
well when they grow up.

Despite the fact that
only one person in
ten is left-handed,

Gerald
Ford

George
Bush

a full third of all
Presidents since 1945
have been left-handed.

Life has not always been
easy for left-handers. From
ancient times until well
into the twentieth century,
left-handedness was looked
upon as a loathsome and
unnatural aberration,
to be dealt with ruthlessly and
with dispatch.

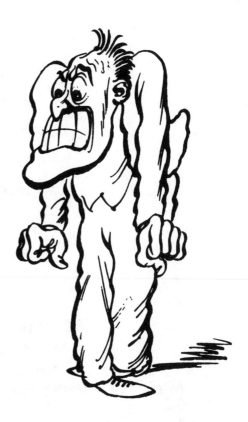

with apologies to
H.M. Bateman

Any child who showed a tendency to favor the left hand was severely chastised by right-minded teachers . . .

. . . cautioned
by right-
minded
parents . . .

. . . lectured by
right-minded
religionists . . .

. . . and vilified by right-minded citizens the world over, who invented self-righteous words to express their approbation of (ugh!) left-handedness.

Given all this social
pressure, most natural
left-handers were
forcibly switched to
right-handers.

Ronald Reagan, who was
born left-handed, was
switched. If he hadn't been
there would have
been still another left-
handed President.

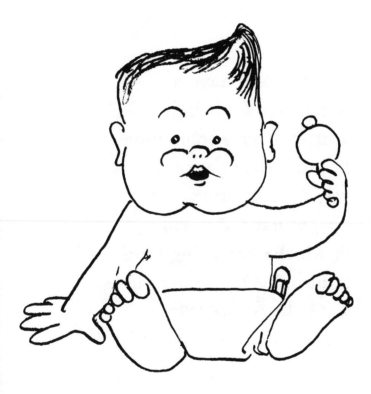

Left-handers have a
reputation for being
a little ditzy. People used
to think they got that
way from coping with
a right-handed world
in which everything from
light bulbs to bottle openers
went the wrong way.

But now we know
that left-handers
are inherently
different from
right-handers.

It's not so much
which hand they use
that makes them
different. It's
which brain.

Scientists have long
known that the human
brain is divided into
two hemispheres, and
that one hemisphere
controls the right hand
and the other controls
the left hand.

But what they've only
recently come to understand
is that the two hemispheres
have entirely different skills,
different personalities, and
different ways of thinking.
Which hand you use
is an indication
of which side of the brain
you're tapped into.

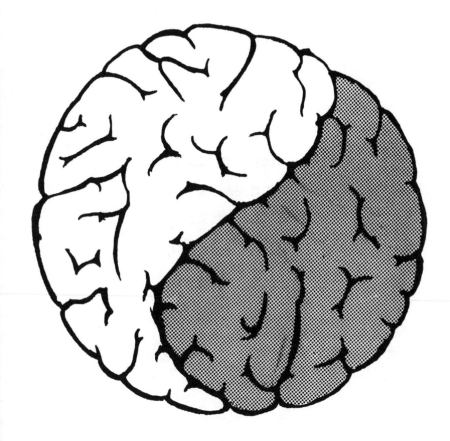

The rational right-handed brain handles words. It contains the basic speech centers and is highly verbal and adept at analytical and sequential thought.

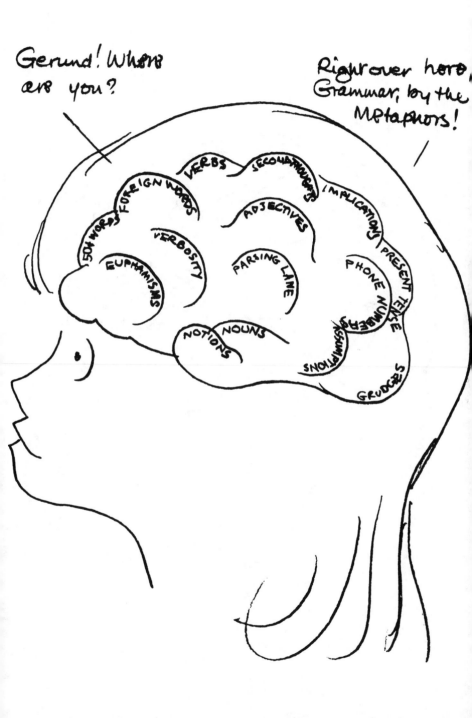

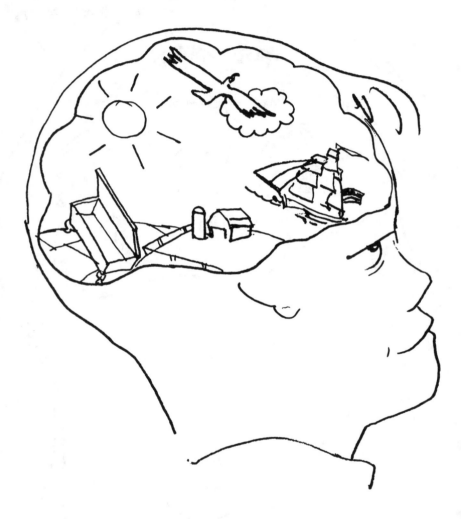

The emotional left-handed
brain thinks in pictures.
It understands three-
dimensional space, music,
tone of voice (but not
words), and is highly
imaginative.

The right-handed brain is good at school because reading, 'riting, and 'rithmetic are all logical, linear disciplines.

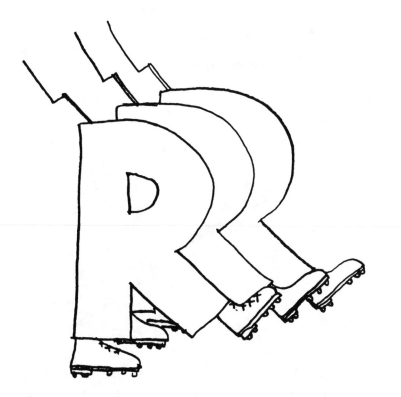

But the left-handed
brain is better at
playing hooky . . .

. . . making
music . . .

. . . drawing
pictures . . .

. . . and telling
jokes.

It's a fact.
Your sense of humor
is in your
left-handed brain.

It's no accident that
so many of the
great comics are
left-handed.

Dick
van
Dyke

Charlie
Chaplin

David
Letterman

W.C.
Fields

Richard
Pryor

Carol
Burnett

Jay
Leno

Marcel
Marceau

Harpo
Marx

Sigmund Freud sensed
the presence of the
left-handed brain, but
because he couldn't
identify it, he labeled
it The Unconscious.

Today we know it's just
as conscious as the
right-handed brain.

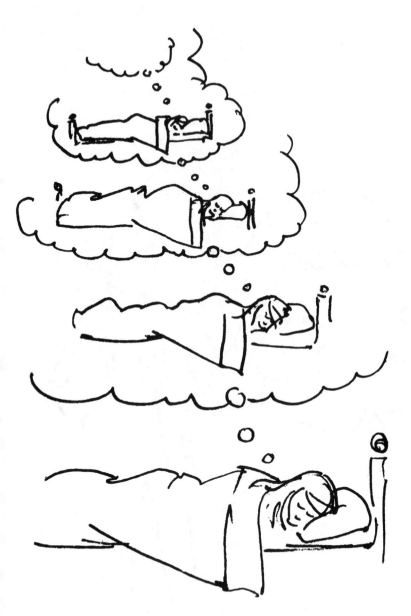

The left-handed brain does most
of our dreaming.

It's also where we get our
"hunches" and other "feelings" that
we can't explain with words.

The left-handed brain
is more susceptible to
alcohol than the
right-handed brain.

Which may explain why
left-handers are more
likely to have
drinking problems.

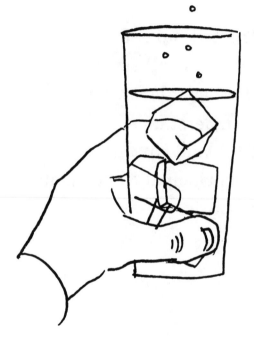

The left-handed
brain has all sorts
of other talents, too.
It understands
pitch and rhythm,
the principal components
of music.

Musical training is a more potent instrument than any other, because rhythm and harmony find their way into the secret places of the soul.

PLATO

Left-handers who
want a job in an
orchestra would do well
to take up the French horn,
which is valved
for the left hand.

But the most
important talent
of the left-handed
brain is
creativity.

Contrary to popular
belief, creativity
has virtually nothing
to do with language
or any of the
intellectual skills
associated with
book-learning.

The basic tools of creative
thinking are mental pictures.
These are handled by the
left-handed brain; and
because it is unhampered
by logic, it is free to
make the kind of
creative connections that
cannot occur in
rational thought.

It is impossible to
think without a
mental picture.
    —Aristotle

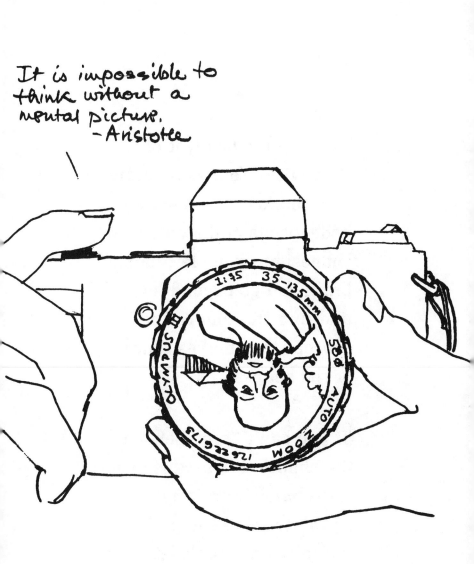

Here's a famous test of creativity. Your noncreative right-handed brain sees only a hodgepodge of disconnected shapes, but your left-handed brain can go beyond logic and find the connecting concept that makes sense of the shapes.

(If you can't "see" beyond the shapes, it's because your right-handed brain is trying to solve the problem logically and won't let your left-handed brain have a go.)

Here's another example, showing
how your left-handed brain
can even create things that
don't exist. It's called
Kanizsa's Triangle.

If you can see the white
triangle—the one with its apex
pointing up—it's because your
left-handed brain has *created*
that triangle to unify what
is otherwise simply a
collection of angles and
Pac Man shapes. There is,
in fact, no white
triangle there.

Michelangelo, who was
left-handed, said "I have
only to throw a pot of
paint on the wall to find
there fine landscapes." What
he was describing, of course,
was his left-handed brain's
wonderful creative ability
to bring order
out of chaos.

The left-handed brain's
mastery of the visual has an
important adjunct—it can "see"
three dimensionally. In Thurston's
Hand Test, you are asked to
identify which pictures are
of left hands and which are of
right hands. Your right-handed
brain is at a loss to handle
this problem, but your left-
handed brain can actually
rotate these drawings in
imaginary space to solve
the test.

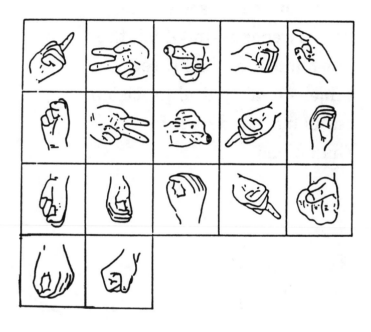

There are some activities—
notably sports—in which the
left-handed brain's three-
dimensional spatial precision
turns left-handers into
champions.

For instance, the
reason there are so many
left-handed tennis stars is
because Borg, Connors,
McEnroe, Navratilova, et al.,
have the ability to predict
precisely where the ball
is going to go.

For the same reason, almost half the major league batting stars, and at least half the pitching stars, are left-handed.

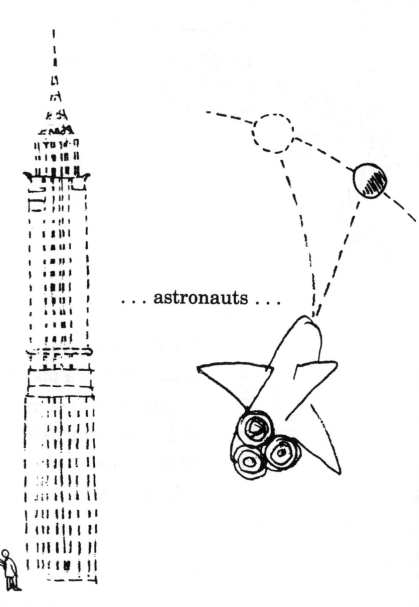

. . . astronauts . . .

Architects . . .

It will be quite an eye-full, eh, monsieur?

. . . and structural engineers are just a few of the other professionals who rely primarily on the three-dimensional left-handed brain.

Ever seen a picture in a
cloud? Or a face in
cracked plaster?

That was your left-handed
brain in the act of
creating.

Is left-handedness
inherited? Possibly.
We know, for instance,
that blond hair is
inherited, and there's a
distinct relationship
between blonds and
left-handedness, as
witness this quartet.

But while there is
some data to
suggest that
left-handedness runs in
families, scientists have
found no hard evidence
that the trait is
carried genetically.

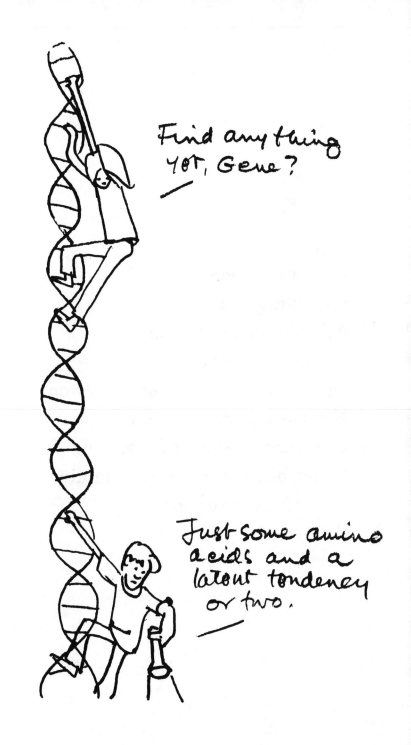

One of the more
intriguing explanations
for left-handedness was
offered by the late
Dr. Norman Geschwind of Boston.
His theories suggest that
handedness is determined long
before birth, and the determining
factor is testosterone,
the male hormone.

It is known that during gestation,
if enough testosterone reaches
the fetus, it will temporarily
inhibit the development of
the right-handed brain,
giving the left-handed brain
a head start.

Result: a left-handed baby.

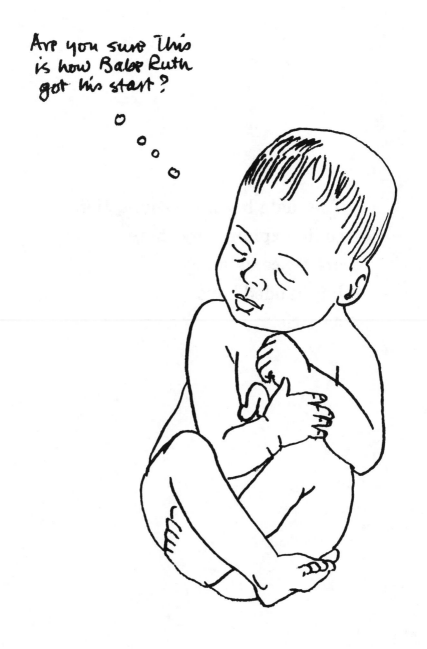

The male hormone connection
could explain why there
are twice as many
left-handed boys
as girls.

Dr. Geschwind's studies
also suggest that
left-handers are more
likely to have allergies
than right-handers.

But they appear to be
less susceptible to
infection and possibly
to certain kinds of
cancer.

No doubt about it—
left-handers are different
from right-handers—
they think differently,
they have different skills,
they even behave differently—
but they are in every way
equal ... and sometimes
maybe superior ... to the
right-handed majority.

What's even more certain
is that for the first time

in history, we are just now
entering the

It's an era when left-handed
thinking is at a premium.

Four of the five designers
of the original Macintosh
computer were left-handed.

It's a time when the law
has ruled that left-handers
have rights, too!

In Woodbridge, Illinois, a jury awarded $136,700 to a left-handed clerk who was ordered to check out groceries with her right hand.

It's a time when
educators have come
to understand the
unique importance
of left-handers.